THIS GARDENING JOURNAL BELONGS TO

_____

_____

_____

CONTACT DETAILS

_____

_____

_____

_____

SUPPLIER CONTACT LIST

COMPANY	STREET	PRODUCTS
WEBSITE	CITY	
EMAIL	STATE	
CONTACT	ZIP CODE	

COMPANY	STREET	PRODUCTS
WEBSITE	CITY	
EMAIL	STATE	
CONTACT	ZIP CODE	

COMPANY	STREET	PRODUCTS
WEBSITE	CITY	
EMAIL	STATE	
CONTACT	ZIP CODE	

COMPANY	STREET	PRODUCTS
WEBSITE	CITY	
EMAIL	STATE	
CONTACT	ZIP CODE	

COMPANY	STREET	PRODUCTS
WEBSITE	CITY	
EMAIL	STATE	
CONTACT	ZIP CODE	

COMPANY	STREET	PRODUCTS
WEBSITE	CITY	
EMAIL	STATE	
CONTACT	ZIP CODE	

SUPPLIER CONTACT LIST

COMPANY		STREET		PRODUCTS
WEBSITE		CITY		
EMAIL		STATE		
CONTACT		ZIP CODE		

COMPANY		STREET		PRODUCTS
WEBSITE		CITY		
EMAIL		STATE		
CONTACT		ZIP CODE		

COMPANY		STREET		PRODUCTS
WEBSITE		CITY		
EMAIL		STATE		
CONTACT		ZIP CODE		

COMPANY		STREET		PRODUCTS
WEBSITE		CITY		
EMAIL		STATE		
CONTACT		ZIP CODE		

COMPANY		STREET		PRODUCTS
WEBSITE		CITY		
EMAIL		STATE		
CONTACT		ZIP CODE		

COMPANY		STREET		PRODUCTS
WEBSITE		CITY		
EMAIL		STATE		
CONTACT		ZIP CODE		

SUPPLIER CONTACT LIST

COMPANY	STREET	PRODUCTS
WEBSITE	CITY	
EMAIL	STATE	
CONTACT	ZIP CODE	

COMPANY	STREET	PRODUCTS
WEBSITE	CITY	
EMAIL	STATE	
CONTACT	ZIP CODE	

COMPANY	STREET	PRODUCTS
WEBSITE	CITY	
EMAIL	STATE	
CONTACT	ZIP CODE	

COMPANY	STREET	PRODUCTS
WEBSITE	CITY	
EMAIL	STATE	
CONTACT	ZIP CODE	

COMPANY	STREET	PRODUCTS
WEBSITE	CITY	
EMAIL	STATE	
CONTACT	ZIP CODE	

COMPANY	STREET	PRODUCTS
WEBSITE	CITY	
EMAIL	STATE	
CONTACT	ZIP CODE	

SUPPLIER CONTACT LIST

COMPANY	STREET	PRODUCTS
WEBSITE	CITY	
EMAIL	STATE	
CONTACT	ZIP CODE	

COMPANY	STREET	PRODUCTS
WEBSITE	CITY	
EMAIL	STATE	
CONTACT	ZIP CODE	

COMPANY	STREET	PRODUCTS
WEBSITE	CITY	
EMAIL	STATE	
CONTACT	ZIP CODE	

COMPANY	STREET	PRODUCTS
WEBSITE	CITY	
EMAIL	STATE	
CONTACT	ZIP CODE	

COMPANY	STREET	PRODUCTS
WEBSITE	CITY	
EMAIL	STATE	
CONTACT	ZIP CODE	

COMPANY	STREET	PRODUCTS
WEBSITE	CITY	
EMAIL	STATE	
CONTACT	ZIP CODE	

SUPPLIER CONTACT LIST

COMPANY	STREET	PRODUCTS
WEBSITE	CITY	
EMAIL	STATE	
CONTACT	ZIP CODE	

COMPANY	STREET	PRODUCTS
WEBSITE	CITY	
EMAIL	STATE	
CONTACT	ZIP CODE	

COMPANY	STREET	PRODUCTS
WEBSITE	CITY	
EMAIL	STATE	
CONTACT	ZIP CODE	

COMPANY	STREET	PRODUCTS
WEBSITE	CITY	
EMAIL	STATE	
CONTACT	ZIP CODE	

COMPANY	STREET	PRODUCTS
WEBSITE	CITY	
EMAIL	STATE	
CONTACT	ZIP CODE	

COMPANY	STREET	PRODUCTS
WEBSITE	CITY	
EMAIL	STATE	
CONTACT	ZIP CODE	

WEATHER LOG

DATE	CODE	TEMPERATURE	HUMIDITY

WEATHER LOG

DATE	CODE	TEMPERATURE	HUMIDITY

WEATHER LOG

DATE	CODE	TEMPERATURE	HUMIDITY

WEATHER LOG

DATE	CODE	TEMPERATURE	HUMIDITY

WEATHER LOG

DATE	CODE	TEMPERATURE	HUMIDITY

WEATHER LOG

DATE	CODE	TEMPERATURE	HUMIDITY

WEATHER LOG

DATE	CODE	TEMPERATURE	HUMIDITY

WEATHER LOG

DATE	CODE	TEMPERATURE	HUMIDITY

WEATHER LOG

DATE	CODE	TEMPERATURE	HUMIDITY

WEATHER LOG

DATE	CODE	TEMPERATURE	HUMIDITY

GARDEN PLOTTING NOTES

GARDEN PLOTTING NOTES

GARDEN PLOTTING NOTES

GARDEN PLOTTING PLAN

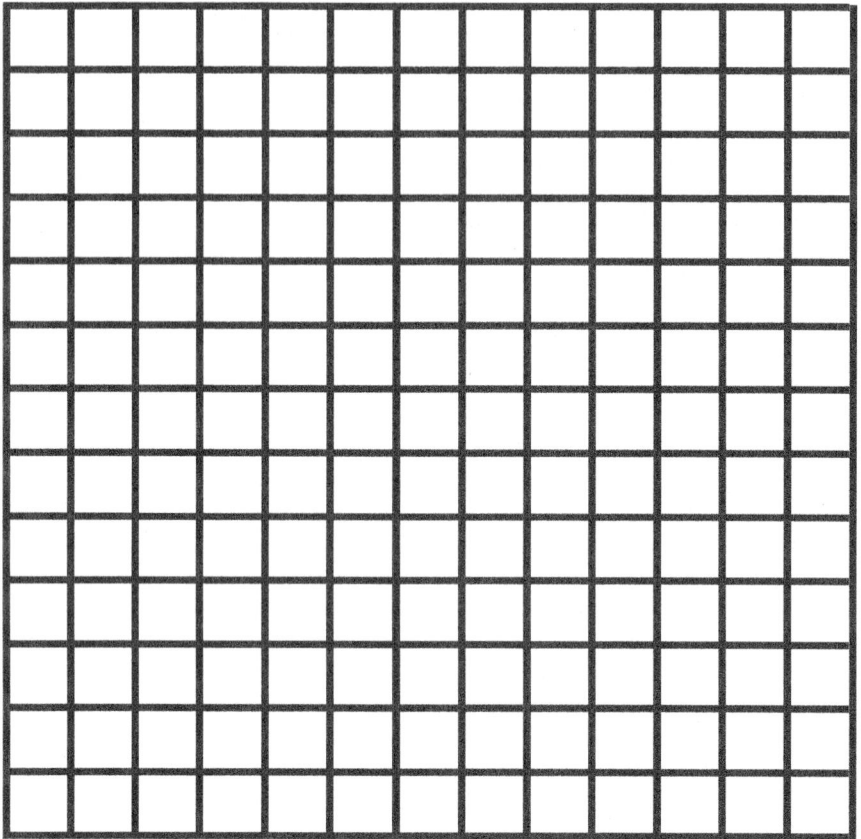

GARDEN PLOTTING PLAN

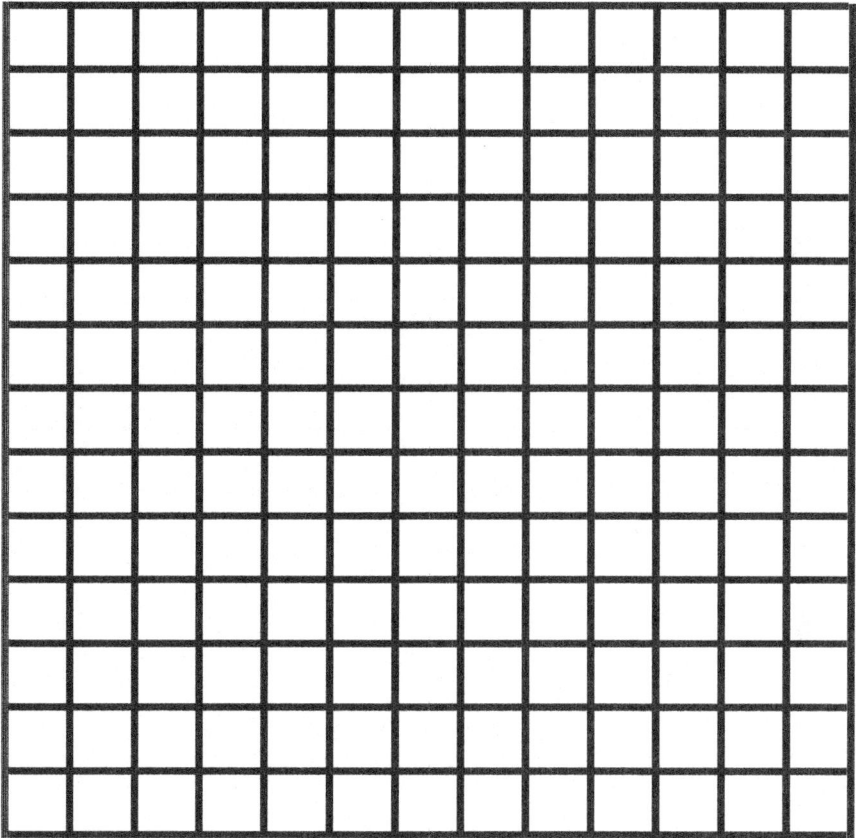

WHEN TO PLANT CHECKLIST

PLANT NAME	J	F	M	A	M	J	J	A	S	O	N	D

WHEN TO PLANT CHECKLIST

PLANT NAME	J	F	M	A	M	J	J	A	S	O	N	D

MONTHLY LOG
JANUARY
WEEK 1

PLANTING	PROPAGATION	PRUNING

MAINTENANCE	PEST CONTROL	OTHER

WEATHER	WILDLIFE

BLOOMS	HIGHLIGHTS

PURCHASED	COST	HARVESTING	AMOUNT

MONTHLY LOG
JANUARY
WEEK 2

PLANTING	PROPAGATION	PRUNING

MAINTENANCE	PEST CONTROL	OTHER

WEATHER	WILDLIFE

BLOOMS	HIGHLIGHTS

PURCHASED	COST	HARVESTING	AMOUNT

MONTHLY LOG
JANUARY
WEEK 3

PLANTING	PROPAGATION	PRUNING

MAINTENANCE	PEST CONTROL	OTHER

WEATHER	WILDLIFE

BLOOMS	HIGHLIGHTS

PURCHASED	COST	HARVESTING	AMOUNT

MONTHLY LOG
JANUARY
WEEK 4

PLANTING	PROPAGATION	PRUNING

MAINTENANCE	PEST CONTROL	OTHER

WEATHER	WILDLIFE

BLOOMS	HIGHLIGHTS

PURCHASED	COST	HARVESTING	AMOUNT

MONTHLY LOG
JANUARY
WEEK 5

PLANTING	PROPAGATION	PRUNING

MAINTENANCE	PEST CONTROL	OTHER

WEATHER	WILDLIFE

BLOOMS	HIGHLIGHTS

PURCHASED	COST	HARVESTING	AMOUNT

MONTHLY LOG
FEBRUARY
WEEK 1

PLANTING	PROPAGATION	PRUNING

MAINTENANCE	PEST CONTROL	OTHER

WEATHER	WILDLIFE

BLOOMS	HIGHLIGHTS

PURCHASED	COST	HARVESTING	AMOUNT

MONTHLY LOG
FEBRUARY
WEEK 2

PLANTING	PROPAGATION	PRUNING

MAINTENANCE	PEST CONTROL	OTHER

WEATHER	WILDLIFE

BLOOMS	HIGHLIGHTS

PURCHASED	COST	HARVESTING	AMOUNT

MONTHLY LOG
FEBRUARY
WEEK 3

PLANTING	PROPAGATION	PRUNING

MAINTENANCE	PEST CONTROL	OTHER

WEATHER	WILDLIFE

BLOOMS	HIGHLIGHTS

PURCHASED	COST	HARVESTING	AMOUNT

MONTHLY LOG
FEBRUARY
WEEK 4

PLANTING	PROPAGATION	PRUNING

MAINTENANCE	PEST CONTROL	OTHER

WEATHER	WILDLIFE

BLOOMS	HIGHLIGHTS

PURCHASED	COST	HARVESTING	AMOUNT

MONTHLY LOG
FEBRUARY
WEEK 5

PLANTING	PROPAGATION	PRUNING

MAINTENANCE	PEST CONTROL	OTHER

WEATHER	WILDLIFE

BLOOMS	HIGHLIGHTS

PURCHASED	COST	HARVESTING	AMOUNT

MONTHLY LOG
MARCH
WEEK 1

PLANTING	PROPAGATION	PRUNING

MAINTENANCE	PEST CONTROL	OTHER

WEATHER	WILDLIFE

BLOOMS	HIGHLIGHTS

PURCHASED	COST	HARVESTING	AMOUNT

MONTHLY LOG
MARCH
WEEK 2

PLANTING	PROPAGATION	PRUNING

MAINTENANCE	PEST CONTROL	OTHER

WEATHER	WILDLIFE

BLOOMS	HIGHLIGHTS

PURCHASED	COST	HARVESTING	AMOUNT

MONTHLY LOG
MARCH
WEEK 3

PLANTING	PROPAGATION	PRUNING

MAINTENANCE	PEST CONTROL	OTHER

WEATHER	WILDLIFE

BLOOMS	HIGHLIGHTS

PURCHASED	COST	HARVESTING	AMOUNT

MONTHLY LOG
MARCH
WEEK 4

PLANTING	PROPAGATION	PRUNING

MAINTENANCE	PEST CONTROL	OTHER

WEATHER	WILDLIFE

BLOOMS	HIGHLIGHTS

PURCHASED	COST	HARVESTING	AMOUNT

MONTHLY LOG
MARCH
WEEK 5

PLANTING	PROPAGATION	PRUNING

MAINTENANCE	PEST CONTROL	OTHER

WEATHER	WILDLIFE

BLOOMS	HIGHLIGHTS

PURCHASED	COST	HARVESTING	AMOUNT

MONTHLY LOG
APRIL
WEEK 1

PLANTING	PROPAGATION	PRUNING

MAINTENANCE	PEST CONTROL	OTHER

WEATHER	WILDLIFE

BLOOMS	HIGHLIGHTS

PURCHASED	COST	HARVESTING	AMOUNT

MONTHLY LOG
APRIL
WEEK 2

PLANTING	PROPAGATION	PRUNING

MAINTENANCE	PEST CONTROL	OTHER

WEATHER	WILDLIFE

BLOOMS	HIGHLIGHTS

PURCHASED	COST	HARVESTING	AMOUNT

MONTHLY LOG
APRIL
WEEK 3

PLANTING	PROPAGATION	PRUNING

MAINTENANCE	PEST CONTROL	OTHER

WEATHER	WILDLIFE

BLOOMS	HIGHLIGHTS

PURCHASED	COST	HARVESTING	AMOUNT

MONTHLY LOG
APRIL
WEEK 4

PLANTING	PROPAGATION	PRUNING

MAINTENANCE	PEST CONTROL	OTHER

WEATHER	WILDLIFE

BLOOMS	HIGHLIGHTS

PURCHASED	COST	HARVESTING	AMOUNT

MONTHLY LOG
APRIL
WEEK 5

PLANTING	PROPAGATION	PRUNING

MAINTENANCE	PEST CONTROL	OTHER

WEATHER	WILDLIFE

BLOOMS	HIGHLIGHTS

PURCHASED	COST	HARVESTING	AMOUNT

MONTHLY LOG
MAY
WEEK 1

PLANTING	PROPAGATION	PRUNING

MAINTENANCE	PEST CONTROL	OTHER

WEATHER	WILDLIFE

BLOOMS	HIGHLIGHTS

PURCHASED	COST	HARVESTING	AMOUNT

MONTHLY LOG
MAY
WEEK 2

PLANTING	PROPAGATION	PRUNING

MAINTENANCE	PEST CONTROL	OTHER

WEATHER	WILDLIFE

BLOOMS	HIGHLIGHTS

PURCHASED	COST	HARVESTING	AMOUNT

MONTHLY LOG
MAY
WEEK 3

PLANTING	PROPAGATION	PRUNING

MAINTENANCE	PEST CONTROL	OTHER

WEATHER	WILDLIFE

BLOOMS	HIGHLIGHTS

PURCHASED	COST	HARVESTING	AMOUNT

MONTHLY LOG
MAY
WEEK 4

PLANTING	PROPAGATION	PRUNING

MAINTENANCE	PEST CONTROL	OTHER

WEATHER	WILDLIFE

BLOOMS	HIGHLIGHTS

PURCHASED	COST	HARVESTING	AMOUNT

MONTHLY LOG
MAY
WEEK 5

PLANTING	PROPAGATION	PRUNING

MAINTENANCE	PEST CONTROL	OTHER

WEATHER	WILDLIFE

BLOOMS	HIGHLIGHTS

PURCHASED	COST	HARVESTING	AMOUNT

MONTHLY LOG
JUNE
WEEK 1

PLANTING	PROPAGATION	PRUNING

MAINTENANCE	PEST CONTROL	OTHER

WEATHER	WILDLIFE

BLOOMS	HIGHLIGHTS

PURCHASED	COST	HARVESTING	AMOUNT

MONTHLY LOG
JUNE
WEEK 2

PLANTING	PROPAGATION	PRUNING

MAINTENANCE	PEST CONTROL	OTHER

WEATHER	WILDLIFE

BLOOMS	HIGHLIGHTS

PURCHASED	COST	HARVESTING	AMOUNT

MONTHLY LOG
JUNE
WEEK 3

PLANTING	PROPAGATION	PRUNING

MAINTENANCE	PEST CONTROL	OTHER

WEATHER	WILDLIFE

BLOOMS	HIGHLIGHTS

PURCHASED	COST	HARVESTING	AMOUNT

MONTHLY LOG
JUNE
WEEK 4

PLANTING	PROPAGATION	PRUNING

MAINTENANCE	PEST CONTROL	OTHER

WEATHER	WILDLIFE

BLOOMS	HIGHLIGHTS

PURCHASED	COST	HARVESTING	AMOUNT

MONTHLY LOG
JUNE
WEEK 5

PLANTING	PROPAGATION	PRUNING

MAINTENANCE	PEST CONTROL	OTHER

WEATHER	WILDLIFE

BLOOMS	HIGHLIGHTS

PURCHASED	COST	HARVESTING	AMOUNT

MONTHLY LOG
JULY
WEEK 1

PLANTING	PROPAGATION	PRUNING

MAINTENANCE	PEST CONTROL	OTHER

WEATHER	WILDLIFE

BLOOMS	HIGHLIGHTS

PURCHASED	COST	HARVESTING	AMOUNT

MONTHLY LOG
JULY
WEEK 2

PLANTING	PROPAGATION	PRUNING

MAINTENANCE	PEST CONTROL	OTHER

WEATHER	WILDLIFE

BLOOMS	HIGHLIGHTS

PURCHASED	COST	HARVESTING	AMOUNT

MONTHLY LOG
JULY
WEEK 3

PLANTING	PROPAGATION	PRUNING

MAINTENANCE	PEST CONTROL	OTHER

WEATHER	WILDLIFE

BLOOMS	HIGHLIGHTS

PURCHASED	COST	HARVESTING	AMOUNT

MONTHLY LOG
JULY
WEEK 4

PLANTING	PROPAGATION	PRUNING

MAINTENANCE	PEST CONTROL	OTHER

WEATHER	WILDLIFE

BLOOMS	HIGHLIGHTS

PURCHASED	COST	HARVESTING	AMOUNT

MONTHLY LOG
JULY
WEEK 5

PLANTING	PROPAGATION	PRUNING

MAINTENANCE	PEST CONTROL	OTHER

WEATHER	WILDLIFE

BLOOMS	HIGHLIGHTS

PURCHASED	COST	HARVESTING	AMOUNT

MONTHLY LOG
AUGUST
WEEK 1

PLANTING	PROPAGATION	PRUNING

MAINTENANCE	PEST CONTROL	OTHER

WEATHER	WILDLIFE

BLOOMS	HIGHLIGHTS

PURCHASED	COST	HARVESTING	AMOUNT

MONTHLY LOG
AUGUST
WEEK 2

PLANTING	PROPAGATION	PRUNING

MAINTENANCE	PEST CONTROL	OTHER

WEATHER	WILDLIFE

BLOOMS	HIGHLIGHTS

PURCHASED	COST	HARVESTING	AMOUNT

MONTHLY LOG
AUGUST
WEEK 3

PLANTING	PROPAGATION	PRUNING

MAINTENANCE	PEST CONTROL	OTHER

WEATHER	WILDLIFE

BLOOMS	HIGHLIGHTS

PURCHASED	COST	HARVESTING	AMOUNT

MONTHLY LOG
AUGUST
WEEK 4

PLANTING	PROPAGATION	PRUNING

MAINTENANCE	PEST CONTROL	OTHER

WEATHER	WILDLIFE

BLOOMS	HIGHLIGHTS

PURCHASED	COST	HARVESTING	AMOUNT

MONTHLY LOG
AUGUST
WEEK 5

PLANTING	PROPAGATION	PRUNING

MAINTENANCE	PEST CONTROL	OTHER

WEATHER	WILDLIFE

BLOOMS	HIGHLIGHTS

PURCHASED	COST	HARVESTING	AMOUNT

MONTHLY LOG
SEPTEMBER
WEEK 1

PLANTING	PROPAGATION	PRUNING

MAINTENANCE	PEST CONTROL	OTHER

WEATHER	WILDLIFE

BLOOMS	HIGHLIGHTS

PURCHASED	COST	HARVESTING	AMOUNT

MONTHLY LOG
SEPTEMBER
WEEK 2

PLANTING	PROPAGATION	PRUNING

MAINTENANCE	PEST CONTROL	OTHER

WEATHER	WILDLIFE

BLOOMS	HIGHLIGHTS

PURCHASED	COST	HARVESTING	AMOUNT

MONTHLY LOG
SEPTEMBER
WEEK 3

PLANTING	PROPAGATION	PRUNING

MAINTENANCE	PEST CONTROL	OTHER

WEATHER	WILDLIFE

BLOOMS	HIGHLIGHTS

PURCHASED	COST	HARVESTING	AMOUNT

MONTHLY LOG
SEPTEMBER
WEEK 4

PLANTING	PROPAGATION	PRUNING

MAINTENANCE	PEST CONTROL	OTHER

WEATHER	WILDLIFE

BLOOMS	HIGHLIGHTS

PURCHASED	COST	HARVESTING	AMOUNT

MONTHLY LOG
SEPTEMBER
WEEK 5

PLANTING	PROPAGATION	PRUNING

MAINTENANCE	PEST CONTROL	OTHER

WEATHER	WILDLIFE

BLOOMS	HIGHLIGHTS

PURCHASED	COST	HARVESTING	AMOUNT

MONTHLY LOG
OCTOBER
WEEK 1

PLANTING	PROPAGATION	PRUNING

MAINTENANCE	PEST CONTROL	OTHER

WEATHER	WILDLIFE

BLOOMS	HIGHLIGHTS

PURCHASED	COST	HARVESTING	AMOUNT

MONTHLY LOG
OCTOBER
WEEK 2

PLANTING	PROPAGATION	PRUNING

MAINTENANCE	PEST CONTROL	OTHER

WEATHER	WILDLIFE

BLOOMS	HIGHLIGHTS

PURCHASED	COST	HARVESTING	AMOUNT

MONTHLY LOG
OCTOBER
WEEK 3

PLANTING	PROPAGATION	PRUNING

MAINTENANCE	PEST CONTROL	OTHER

WEATHER	WILDLIFE

BLOOMS	HIGHLIGHTS

PURCHASED	COST	HARVESTING	AMOUNT

MONTHLY LOG
OCTOBER
WEEK 4

PLANTING	PROPAGATION	PRUNING

MAINTENANCE	PEST CONTROL	OTHER

WEATHER	WILDLIFE

BLOOMS	HIGHLIGHTS

PURCHASED	COST	HARVESTING	AMOUNT

MONTHLY LOG
OCTOBER
WEEK 5

PLANTING	PROPAGATION	PRUNING

MAINTENANCE	PEST CONTROL	OTHER

WEATHER	WILDLIFE

BLOOMS	HIGHLIGHTS

PURCHASED	COST	HARVESTING	AMOUNT

MONTHLY LOG
NOVEMBER
WEEK 1

PLANTING	PROPAGATION	PRUNING

MAINTENANCE	PEST CONTROL	OTHER

WEATHER	WILDLIFE

BLOOMS	HIGHLIGHTS

PURCHASED	COST	HARVESTING	AMOUNT

MONTHLY LOG
NOVEMBER
WEEK 2

PLANTING	PROPAGATION	PRUNING

MAINTENANCE	PEST CONTROL	OTHER

WEATHER	WILDLIFE

BLOOMS	HIGHLIGHTS

PURCHASED	COST	HARVESTING	AMOUNT

MONTHLY LOG
NOVEMBER
WEEK 3

PLANTING	PROPAGATION	PRUNING

MAINTENANCE	PEST CONTROL	OTHER

WEATHER	WILDLIFE

BLOOMS	HIGHLIGHTS

PURCHASED	COST	HARVESTING	AMOUNT

MONTHLY LOG
NOVEMBER
WEEK 4

PLANTING	PROPAGATION	PRUNING

MAINTENANCE	PEST CONTROL	OTHER

WEATHER	WILDLIFE

BLOOMS	HIGHLIGHTS

PURCHASED	COST	HARVESTING	AMOUNT

MONTHLY LOG
NOVEMBER
WEEK 5

PLANTING	PROPAGATION	PRUNING

MAINTENANCE	PEST CONTROL	OTHER

WEATHER	WILDLIFE

BLOOMS	HIGHLIGHTS

PURCHASED	COST	HARVESTING	AMOUNT

MONTHLY LOG
DECEMBER
WEEK 1

PLANTING	PROPAGATION	PRUNING

MAINTENANCE	PEST CONTROL	OTHER

WEATHER	WILDLIFE

BLOOMS	HIGHLIGHTS

PURCHASED	COST	HARVESTING	AMOUNT

MONTHLY LOG
DECEMBER
WEEK 2

PLANTING	PROPAGATION	PRUNING

MAINTENANCE	PEST CONTROL	OTHER

WEATHER	WILDLIFE

BLOOMS	HIGHLIGHTS

PURCHASED	COST	HARVESTING	AMOUNT

MONTHLY LOG
DECEMBER
WEEK 3

PLANTING	PROPAGATION	PRUNING

MAINTENANCE	PEST CONTROL	OTHER

WEATHER	WILDLIFE

BLOOMS	HIGHLIGHTS

PURCHASED	COST	HARVESTING	AMOUNT

MONTHLY LOG
DECEMBER
WEEK 4

PLANTING	PROPAGATION	PRUNING

MAINTENANCE	PEST CONTROL	OTHER

WEATHER	WILDLIFE

BLOOMS	HIGHLIGHTS

PURCHASED	COST	HARVESTING	AMOUNT

MONTHLY LOG
DECEMBER
WEEK 5

PLANTING	PROPAGATION	PRUNING

MAINTENANCE	PEST CONTROL	OTHER

WEATHER	WILDLIFE

BLOOMS	HIGHLIGHTS

PURCHASED	COST	HARVESTING	AMOUNT

Printed in Great Britain
by Amazon

57410752R00051